Anonymous

Banquet to the Honored Whitelaw Reid

Minister of the United States to France in 1892

Anonymous

Banquet to the Honored Whitelaw Reid
Minister of the United States to France in 1892

ISBN/EAN: 9783337339234

Printed in Europe, USA, Canada, Australia, Japan

Cover: Foto ©Suzi / pixelio.de

More available books at **www.hansebooks.com**

CHAMBER OF COMMERCE

OF THE

STATE OF NEW-YORK.

BANQUET

TO THE

Hon. WHITELAW REID,

MINISTER OF THE UNITED STATES TO FRANCE.

DELMONICO'S, SATURDAY, APRIL 16TH, 1892.

NEW-YORK:
PRESS OF THE CHAMBER OF COMMERCE.

1892.

CONTENTS.

————•——

BANQUET

TO THE

HON. WHITELAW REID

Minister of the United States to France

Upon the announcement of the approaching return of
the Hon. WHITELAW REID from his mission as Minister
of the United States to France, and in view of his important diplomatic achievement in the opening of the
markets of that nation to one of the most important of
American products, as well as the negotiation of an Extradition Treaty with that power, steps were taken by
the Chamber of Commerce to show, by some unusual
demonstration, the appreciation in which such services
are held. Accordingly the Executive Committee of the
Chamber, on the 7th of April, reported the following
preamble and resolutions for adoption :

Whereas, The Hon. WHITELAW REID, our esteemed
friend and distinguished fellow-citizen, has returned to
this city from France, to which nation he is the Minister
of the United States ; and

Whereas, In that high service he has shown diplomatic qualities of the first order in the negotiation of a
Reciprocity Treaty which opens the large market of

that prosperous Republic to one of the most important of American products ; and further, in the arrangement of an Extradition Treaty to protect the people of our respective countries from the criminal classes of either ; and

Whereas, His services as Minister of the United States have been here and abroad recognized as of great value in securing the proper representation of our people at the Paris Exposition of 1889, and more lately in the provision for a similar adequate representation of French interests at the Columbian Exposition in 1893 ; and

Whereas, By his culture, his personal dignity and his urbanity he has won the esteem of the official dignitaries of the nation to which he is accredited, and by his kind solicitude for their interests the affection of our own people resident or visiting abroad ; therefore,

Resolved, That this Chamber, in appreciation of this service and character, tender him a Banquet of welcome to his home and country at such time as may suit his convenience.

Resolved, Further, that Mr. REID be and he is hereby nominated and recommended for election as an Honorary member of this Chamber.

The preamble and resolutions were adopted by acclamation, and Mr. REID was unanimously elected an Honorary member.

A Committee was thereupon appointed to take charge and carry out the details of the Banquet. This Committee consisted of the following named gentlemen :

CORNELIUS N. BLISS,   CHAUNCEY M. DEPEW,
SAMUEL D. BABCOCK,   HORACE PORTER,
ALEXANDER E. ORR.

Mr. REID accepted the courtesy of the Chamber, and the Banquet was given at DELMONICO's on Saturday evening, April 16th. The occasion brought together a large representation of New-York's most distinguished merchants and business men, with the following guests :

The Hon. WHITELAW REID, Minister of the United States to France.
Governor WILLIAM R. MERRIAM, of Minnesota.
The Hon. CALVIN S. BRICE.
The Hon. FRANK HISCOCK.
The Hon. CARL SCHURZ.
The Hon. CHARLES A. DANA.
President SETH LOW, of Columbia College.
The Hon. MURAT HALSTEAD.
Mr. FREDERIC R. COUDERT.
The Rev. JAMES H. McILVAINE, D. D.
The Rev. JOHN W. BROWN, D. D.
The Hon. STEWART L. WOODFORD.
Mr. DAVID M. STONE.
Mr. ISAAC H. BROMLEY.
Mr. D. O. MILLS.
Mr. ARTHUR F. BOWERS.
Mr. HENRY HALL.
Mr. HART LYMAN.
Mr. EDWARD CARY.
Mr. ST. CLAIR McKELWAY.
Mr. JOHN A. SCHLEICHER.
Mr. OGDEN MILLS.
Mr. HENRY P. SAMPERS.
Mr. JAMES PHILLIPS, Jr.

Mr. CHARLES S. SMITH, President of the Chamber of Commerce, presided.

Grace was said by the Rev. JOHN W. BROWN, D. D.

The President, upon introducing the Hon. WHITELAW

REID, the guest of the evening, noticed the fact that in the entire course of the existence of the Chamber the distinction of honorary membership had only been conferred by it on twenty-four persons, and each of those of the highest merit. He laid stress upon the peculiar propriety of thus honoring Mr. REID, whose services to commerce had been of exceeding value in the successful negotiation with France of two important treaties.

The first toasts were becoming the occasion, being to the President of the United States and the President of the Republic of France. The French Minister not being present, the compliment to France was acknowledged by Mr. FREDERIC R. COUDERT.

In his speech he alluded gracefully to the early sympathy of that great nation for the Western Republic, struggling into life, and her early adoption of the principles of democracy first vindicated in its successful establishment.

He also alluded to the Presidents of the two Republics as the real representatives of the new political and social civilization thus inaugurated, and to President CARNOT as descendant of one of those who shaped the beginnings of this civilization in France.

President HARRISON holds the same relation to one of the founders of the American Republic.

He closed with the expression of an abiding faith in the permanent establishment of democracy in France, and the maintenance of peace, which is the true mission of Republics.

The guest of the evening, the Hon. WHITELAW REID, was welcomed with enthusiasm.

In his address he was abundant in his appreciation of the honors conferred upon him in this special reception of the merchants of New-York, the commercial centre of the continent, and his admission as honorary member to the ranks of their representative body.

He modestly disclaimed any credit for the authorship

of the policy which he had successfully carried out in France, saying that it was the policy of the President of the United States and of the Secretary of State, to the lines of which he had strictly confined himself.

He believed that it was a policy which would result to the mutual benefit of both nations, and what there was of diplomatic achievement was equally to be credited to the friendly disposition of the French officials.

Mr. DANA, whose editorial training was received in the office of *The Tribune*, where Mr. REID now fills the honored chair held by its founder, Mr. GREELEY, sat on the left of the President, as the representative of the press, in whose service Mr. REID also achieved his first distinction, and after Mr. REID'S happy and eloquent response to the toast, the "Guest of the Evening," Mr. DANA responded congratulating Mr. REID on the invaluable service he had rendered the United States in securing a mutual agreement with France, as to the admission of their products. General HORACE PORTER completed the words of compliment in a witty speech on "Modern Diplomacy, the Ally of Commerce."

President SETH LOW, of Columbia College, made a brief address on the purposes of diplomacy, and the fitness of the editor for its positions. He recalled his own experience as a merchant with French tradesmen, and complimented them upon their superior artistic taste in manufacture, which he attributed chiefly to the fact that France throws her art schools open to all the world.

The proceedings were closed by the Hon. MURAT HALSTEAD, a distinguished member of the press and an old intimate personal friend of the guest of the evening, in a few words congratulatory to Mr. REID on his well earned honors in a new field of national usefulness.

SPEECH OF MR. CHARLES S. SMITH, PRESIDENT OF THE
CHAMBER OF COMMERCE.

GENTLEMEN : As I look into your faces I am sure
that you share with me the pleasure I have in congratulating our friend and guest upon the presence of so
many of his warm personal friends, whose respect,
admiration and affection he has so worthily won.
While the charms of social ties always have special
attraction, and contribute much to lighten and sweeten
the burdens of life, still it is not the possession of
these admirable qualities alone on the part of our guest
which has brought together this distinguished company
of representative citizens in honor of the United States
Minister to our sister Republic of France.

During the century and a quarter of the existence of
the Chamber of Commerce, its honorary membership
has been conferred but twenty-four times. I trust you
will not conclude that I am using an extravagant expression when I say that the honor roll of the Chamber
is the American merchant's patent of nobility. [Ap-
plause.] "The Iron Cross" of American commerce.
This marked expression of the obligation of the Chamber
to Mr. REID was conferred upon him because he has
conducted his high office with conspicuous ability and
fidelity to the interests of American commerce, and
with a view to the promotion of American ideas and
traditions. [Applause.]

Mr. REID has enlarged and strengthened the historic
friendship of France for this country. [Applause.] He
has cemented the relations which are consecrated in our
memories by the illustrious names of WASHINGTON and
LAFAYETTE, of MIRABEAU and FRANKLIN.

It is within the bounds of truth to say, that at no time
in our history has the genuine good will and mutual
esteem of the two great countries been so intimate and

reciprocal as at this moment. [Applause.] I know from personal observation something of the difficulties which Mr. REID had to encounter, and which, by patient industry and diplomatic tact, he surmounted, and which, (to paraphrase a witty saying of Mr. PHELPS, at Berlin,) led to the triumphant entry of the American pig, under the shadow of the Arc de Triomphe, into the markets of France. [Laughter and applause.] Let us hope that the products of Chicago and Cincinnati will nourish the stomach of the Frenchman and enlarge the pockets of the American, and so illustrate true commercial reciprocity. [Laughter and applause.]

Our guest is still young, and to him fame came early with her laurel wreath of power. Perhaps one of the secrets of that power was in his early experience and training under that great master of journalism, HORACE GREELEY. [Applause.] It has been in the line of Mr. REID's profession as a public censor to receive blows as well as to give them, and he possesses the enviable ability to do this with such courtesy as to command the respect and retain the friendship of all good men, and of all parties. [Applause.]

Now, gentlemen, please fill your glasses and drink to the first regular toast : "THE PRESIDENT OF THE UNITED STATES." [The entire assemblage arose and remained standing, while the orchestra played "The Star Spangled Banner."]

The President then announced the next regular toast : "THE PRESIDENT OF THE REPUBLIC OF FRANCE." [The "Marseillaise" hymn was played by the orchestra.]

THE PRESIDENT.—Gentlemen, there is no man in the United States, in the absence of the French Minister, better fitted to respond to this sentiment than our distinguished fellow-citizen, FREDERIC R. COUDERT. Although by birth an American, he inherits the grace and wit so characteristic of the country to which he owes his name. [Applause.] I now call upon Mr. COUDERT to respond.

SPEECH OF MR. FREDERIC R. COUDERT.

MR. PRESIDENT: It was once said with little exaggeration, that when France had a cold in her head, the rest of Europe sneezed. An epigrammatic tribute, I take it, to her genius, her power and perhaps her restlessness; or rather to that overflowing activity of life that would not be restrained by narrow geographical or political limitations, but must look abroad for moral and sometimes physical conquests to satisfy the cravings of exuberant health. No disease could touch her that did not move the world to ready and sympathetic unrest. How could it be else? Was she not the mother of civilization, the queen of the arts, the champion of every great and generous cause? The tramp of her victorious armies had been heard with almost wearisome monotony on every battlefield of Europe from Charlemagne to Saint Louis; from Saint Louis to Louis XIV.; from LOUIS XIV. to NAPOLEON. What a record of heroism; what a catalogue of heroes. [Applause.] And as she pursued her career of moral and physical triumphs she effaced the traces of war with the same hand that smote; for she sowed the seed of a glorious democracy while her philosophers, scientists and literary men prepared the way for the brotherhood of Nations. Who can gainsay her title to the gratitude of mankind? I need not rehearse her claims nor produce her witnesses before an American tribunal. Her blood, her treasure, her sympathy; she spent all that she had to make American liberty her debtor. Your honored guest will tell you that the tenderness that she once lavished on

America she has never taken back. [Applause.] Whether or not that love has been fully or constantly requited, whether in the dark hours of desolation, when she wept in sackcloth and ashes and refused to be comforted because her children were not, whether in the hour of humiliation her brethren of America heard her voice and wiped her tears, why should we ask? *She* never did. Her trust and affection were always as of old. Whatever else she might question she could not doubt that those who honored WASHINGTON would mourn with the bereaved countrymen of LAFAYETTE. She comforted her bruised heart, in sore defeat, by remembering the trials and sufferings that culminated in the common glory of Yorktown. So long as fortune could not obliterate the records of the past, the jewel of American love and sympathy must be hers forever. And then while still weak from loss of blood and soiled with the dust of defeat, she raised the torch of liberty, and, waving it that the world might be gladdened by its rays, she called America to witness that there was a new bond between the two nations. [Applause.] Thus did she consecrate the old allegiance by a gift embodying the glories and triumphs of the past, the union of the present and the aspirations of the future.

The President of the French Republic! What a title, what an opportunity, what a burden! To direct the destinies of the nation that knew RICHELIEU and HENRY IV., LOUIS XIV. and NAPOLEON, to be the foremost man in a nation of thirty-six million gallant people, to represent before the world her rights, to be responsible for the performance of her duties, to see that no detriment shall befall the young Republic that has fallen heir to such priceless treasures! This is no light task. He must remain faithful to sacred memories and march to the music of a brilliant future. He must be the pioneer of the people in the emancipation of thought and the development of freedom. He will, if faithful to his trust and equal to its performance, justify great expectations and fulfil great prophecies. A heavy task this to fall on one man's shoulders ! The Republican President who lives in Paris, and the Republican President who lives in Washington, with 100,000,000 people behind them, are the real representatives of the new civilization. To them is committed the standard of all that is best in modern progress.

The President of the French Republic bears a name well fitted to commend him to his people's affections. In the battle for freedom that began a century ago the great CARNOT was at his post and faithful to his duty. History reports his unflinching fidelity to Republican principles as one of his claims to the gratitude of posterity, but history clothes him with a far stronger title to posthumous veneration. He was a Republican, it is true, but, first and always, he was a patriot. The love of country was stronger than the love of party or the scruple of consistency. We, who have heard the echo of WASHINGTON's voice warning us against the destructive potency of party spirit as the danger most likely to disrupt our union, may uncover in reverent homage to the CARNOT of the French Republic, the organizer of victory. It was the same CARNOT who dropped and brushed aside his personal preferences to join hands in patriotic forgetfulness of self with the tottering NAPOLEON of 1814. For that NAPOLEON, whatever the blemishes upon his matchless genius, then incarnated in his person, though his star was on the wane, the traditions, the honor, the patriotism of France. It was no time for ponderous Senates to discuss nice questions of constitutional law, nor to dilate in sonorous periods upon the abstract blessings of civil liberty. The enemy were thundering at the gates, the soil was trodden and polluted by the invader, the grim warriors of Marengo, Austerlitz and Moscow were doing their heroic duty, but melting away before the swarms of their united enemies.

Then the patriot CARNOT hastened to the side of the lion at bay, and urged his countrymen to forget all things except the insulted land of their fathers. "Ah, CARNOT!" said the Emperor, "I have known you too late!" And yet, when he was the manufacturer of Royalty and the master of a continent he had said to this same CARNOT: "You may have all that you want, as you want, and when you want." But the stern Republican was not then bound to yield allegiance to the man who had brushed aside the Republic. The hour came with the nation's humiliation, and he only proffered his service when it could not be rewarded. Well might the German NEIBUHR, glowing with admiration at this heroic and patriotic citizen's deeds, declare: "If all that I had in the world were a crust of bread, I should be proud to share it with CARNOT."

And now the grandson is the chief magistrate of the nation that NAPOLEON ruled and covered with renown. [Applause.] Is he worthy of this conspicuous honor, and may we hope that his hands will hold up the dignity and prosperity of his people? The years of his probation have answered the question. It has been the rare good fortune of the Republic to find among her citizens a man who knew how to fill this exalted part. [Applause.] Happy the people who possess the man required for their emergency; happier still the people who esteem him at his worth and honor him accordingly. Party differences are subdued and silent when he challenges judgment. The people know him and repel partisan criticism of their faithful servant. For such he is, and such they know him to be. No craving for a wider sphere of uncontrolled action, no selfish hope of personal aggrandizement have ever marred his conduct or dimmed his fame. He has learned, perhaps, from the traditions of his household, that the first citizen of France is simply the most honored servant of the people; that the duty of a President is to execute the laws, not to make them ; that the function of his office is to enlighten the nation, not to endanger its peace or to destroy the liberties of his people. The President of the French Republic is the pedagogue of Europe. His chair is a pulpit whence he is to teach that liberty means light, that she carries the book and the pen where she may, the sword only where she must; that his first duty is to teach obedience to the law, by practicing it ; to accept, not to dictate, to be vigilant and true and honest and brave in his allegiance to the Sovereign, for the law is his master, even when he reviews one hundred thousand men.

Truisms, these things seem to us. A successor of President WASHINGTON who would dream of usurping the power confided to his hands, and of placing himself above the laws, could hardly hope for anything more serious from an American audience than to be hissed off the stage. More probably a continent would shake with laughter, and a performance intended to be dramatic would end in burlesque. The American people are not without a sense of humor, though it is often inadequately expressed. There are springs in their intellectual make-up that may be touched with effect, and they would rise to all the requirements of a mirth-provoking situation if any citizen, whether in the White House or out of it, should act upon the theory that he was indispensable to the welfare of the nation. The Saviour of Society has no place here. He is not classed among our vertebrated animals, and the popular diagnosis would at once recognize the presence of mental disease. Hellebore was the reputed cure in the old Roman days ; the strait jacket or mild confinement is the more modern method. But we have not ten millions of armed men in our close proximity, most of whom may, in the chances of diplomacy or accident, be our enemies to-morrow. The waves and fogs and storms of the Atlantic are the steady and inexpensive bulwarks of our main frontier, and as to other possible foes—but we have none. [Applause.]

Not so, however, in the old land of France. The man on horseback still lives in legend and tradition. He has done great things in days gone by, and may perhaps forget that he is no longer a factor in the peaceful destinies of the country. One thousand years of unremitting activity have surely earned the right to repose. Glory may have its uses, but glory palls in time upon the taste, and its music loses all charm for modern ears. France wants a leader who will tap the boundless resources of her genius for the pursuits of peace. He must insist that he shall freely extend the new domain that she has chosen for herself. True, a shadow is still on the wall, and the day may come when her children shall be summoned again to try the cruel chances of war. But, should the fated day come, which may Heaven avert, she will remember that of her fathers, the Gauls, it was said by their Roman foes that they did not fear funerals. This is a sombre theme, and we all prefer to watch her growth in the field of her own selection, the arts and sciences and literature that adorn and delight and bless our race.

Honor then to this, her chief magistrate. May he succeed in his mission of peace. The experiment of free government is being made by a nation under whose soil lie sleeping fifty generations of men; they were born and bred under a system that made one man better, by accident of birth, than all other men; what wonder if she has not, at one bound, mastered the excellencies of a wholly different scheme. The habits of a nation may not be shaken off in a day. Nor, on the other hand, must we forget that democracy and republicanism are not convertible terms. France has been for a century the most democratic of nations. As one of our own great leaders of thought once said: True democracy does not consist in saying, I am as good as you, but rather in saying, you are as good as I. She knows this lesson by heart. True republicanism. consists in obeying equal laws with ready and cheerful alacrity. Why should not the young Republic live up to this simple canon of republican conduct? Adversity has bowed the head of her people in humiliation and sorrow. It were idle to deny that old wounds are not quite healed, or that retrospection is unmixed with bitterness. But the nation has turned its face to the light of a new dawn. Another generation is coming forward that will be slow to abandon the fruits of their fathers' trials, and will readily be taught that liberty is better than servitude ; that it is better to be a citizen than to be a subject ; that to serve one's country is better than to serve a king. We of America may be pardoned if we rejoice in that belief and exult in our possession. May we not hope that the old nation, who was our friend when we sorely needed friends, may join hands with us, not for selfish purposes and selfish aggrandizement, but for the benefit of the human race? [Applause.] Made up as we are of so composite a texture, representing every nation of the world, because each one contributed from its best citizens to our prosperity, we may truly say that nothing that interests mankind is foreign to us.

And in drinking the health of the honored President of the French Republic we will, with grateful recollections and renewed affection, pledge the fair land that still lives in undiminished brilliancy to instruct and charm the world. [Loud and continued applause.]

The President here announced the letters of regret received from gentlemen who were prevented from attending the Banquet. These letters will be found at the close of these pages.

THE PRESIDENT.—Gentlemen, the next regular toast

is : "THE GUEST OF THE CHAMBER OF COMMERCE, THE HON. WHITELAW REID." Let us now drink to his health and continued prosperity.

When Mr. REID arose to respond, he was greeted with the strongest proof of the friendship entertained for him by the merchants of New-York, and, after the cheering had subsided, he spoke as follows:

SPEECH OF THE HON. WHITELAW REID, MINISTER OF THE UNITED STATES TO FRANCE.

MR. PRESIDENT : Now I know that I am at home. [Applause.] That old refrain and those American cheers tell the story. I accept your words used a little while ago. The approval of the New-York Chamber of Commerce, given to a townsman returning from the service of his country abroad, is a decoration. [Applause.] Your electing him to the little group of your honorary members does confer more than ribbons and crosses and jewelled orders. [Applause.]

No man knows better than your guest what and how much it means ; and if, in a fortnight at home, renewed and persistent kindnesses had not made him a very beggar for words, no man could more sincerely or more gratefully thank you. Outside of politics and religion, to a New-Yorker, little is left unsaid when the Chamber of Commerce has spoken. In a letter of remarkable candor, which appeared the other day in the morning journals, a distinguished citizen, who has held the highest office in the gift of his countrymen, wrote with honest simplicity that he often feared he did not deserve all the kind things said of him. Under favor of that example, I may venture to say that I have often experienced the same feeling. I wish I could believe that I deserve what you say ; but the net result of it all is, a sense, not of increased importance, but of the increasing necessity for more than my natural modesty. [Applause.]

And yet there is one point, Mr. President, on which I accept very frankly and very honestly all your eulogium. I have tried to do my full duty to this great city, and to the great country behind it, which I had the honor to represent near the Government of our earliest European friend. [Applause and cheers.]

My difficulties there were largely lessened and my power for any useful service increased from my having had the good fortune to be supported by my countrymen without distinction of party. It is his high incentive to duty, and, indeed, the inspiration of his office, that the American Minister represents no party, however glorious its record, or however devoted his attachment to it; but that like RICHELIEU, in the elder BULWER'S play, with the receipt of his commission there has entered his official veins the power, the dignity, the honor of the whole sixty-five millions of people, of the magnificent continent they inhabit, and the matchless history they inherit. [Applause.]

It has been another comfort for your Minister in Paris during the past three years to find himself still among his own countrymen. Naturally a Minister from New-York is likely to see more friends and acquaintances in Paris than a representative of any other locality. But the truth is, that American friends so surrounded and supported the Paris Legation, from the first day of my incumbency to the last, that I was scarcely ever left reason to realize that I was far from City Hall Square or Fifth Avenue or Pennsylvania Avenue. [Applause.]

And now, Mr. President, I wish, if not to discharge, at least to acknowledge, my heaviest obligation. I wish to tender my best thanks to my own profession, the Press, for the uniform and considerate kindness with which it has treated me, without distinction of parties and without exception. This was as it ought to be, for a Minister in a foreign Nation, representing his whole country, is entitled to its whole support, or to immediate recall. But in my case there has been a spontaneity about it and a generosity, alike from old friends and old enemies, which touched me to the heart's core. There has been in it, too, a species of comradeship most grateful to a man who has held every place in the ranks, from the lowest, and who prizes, above all other honors, the distinction conferred by the good will and esteem of his colleagues and rivals in his own calling. [Applause.]

If there has been any success at the Paris Legation in the past three years to warrant this great kindness of the press, and this distinguished honor your Chamber now bestows, it is due, first of all, to BENJAMIN HARRISON and JAMES G. BLAINE. They determined their policy and stuck to it. They gave me their instructions, and then gave me unquestioning confidence and support, and left me a free hand. The man who, under those circumstances, cannot do good work, has no good work in him. [Applause.]

But with reference to any diplomatic success, I am reminded of what seemed to me a very sagacious remark, made not long ago by Lord SALISBURY, to the effect that, while it was desirable to carry your points in diplomacy as far as possible, it was equally desirable not to brag about it afterwards. [Laughter and applause.] The other Nation might thus be led to think it had conceded too much ; and so, in the end, the brag might undo the diplomacy. The counsel is good for us now and always ; though in the present case there can be no such danger, since most of the agreements have been confessedly in the common interest—as all of them were, in our opinion—and since the only ones about which a difference of judgment as to actual interest could exist were in the furtherance of an absolute justice, to our demand for which no adequate reason for refusal ever had been or ever could be given.

May I be pardoned for reading, as appropriate to this view of our diplomacy, the charming words in which the great French orator, Senator and Academician, as well as newspaper writer, M. JULES SIMON, closed his good-bye to me, three weeks ago, at a banquet in Paris.

(The following is the text of M. SIMON's concluding sentences. Mr. REID held the Paris paper in his hand, but merely turned it into English, as below :

"Vous allez partir, Monsieur REID, mais vouz laissez ici des amis qui ne vous oublieront pas. Lorsque le paquebot qui vous emportera vers le Nouveau Monde quittera les côtes de France, je voudrais être sur le promontoire le plus avancé de ces côtes, et je vous crierai dans un dernier écho. Répandons la liberté avec la lumiére : répandons la justice avec la liberté.")

"When the vessel which carries you toward the New World shall quit the coasts of France, I should like to be on the promontory the most advanced of these coasts, and would cry to you then in a last echo, from our land to yours, let us spread liberty with the light ; let us spread justice with liberty." [Laughter and cheers.]

Well, gentlemen, your President has referred to what my friend, Mr. PHELPS, has grotesquely styled the passage of the American pig under the Arc de Triomphe. The animal didn't get in very quickly, and he didn't get in very easily ; but in the language which the West has made classic, he got there. [Laughter.]

The absolute prohibition of American pork in France lasted eleven years. It was an invidious discrimination, since it touched only the United States, and it was defended and screened from the charge of distinct unfriendliness only on the ground that the American product was dangerous to the public health. At the same time, importations were permitted from other countries, in at least one of which trichinosis was notoriously abundant and fatal. It must not be forgotten that, from the long time prohibition had lasted, as well as from the charges on which it had been ordered, the great mass of the French people honestly believed it to be needful ; while there were three powerful classes absolutely sure of it—the French pork-growers, the French pork-packers and the Protectionists ; and they had overwhelming majorities in Parliament. Let me say at once, that the diplomatic contest was ended as soon as the case had been fully presented. When the judgment of the French Government was convinced, it was instantly ready to do right. What remained was a question of convincing the Chambers, also, and of adjusting duties on the general scale then about to be adopted in their new tariff. On that point, as you know, legislators on both sides of the water are apt to have views of their own. [Laughter.]

I had the pleasure of bringing home an extradition treaty, completed in the last week of my stay and signed on the day of my departure. It will be of some interest to the merchants of New-York, for it more than doubles the number of extraditable crimes with France. And if the Senate should now kindly take the same benevolent view of it with its authors, and confirm it promptly, it may have the effect of making the crimes which peculiarly harass the merchant more rare among you, and Paris less attractive to any Americans except the good ones. [Laughter.]

A limited commercial agreement, which I had the pleasure of closing just before my return, and in which the Chamber will take some interest, has not yet been proclaimed by the President, since it needs first the assent of the French Chambers. The Tariff Commission has reported, however, unanimously in its favor, and the French Ministers seemed to have no doubt about its approval. Here, coming under Section 3 of the new

Tariff Bill, it requires no ratification by the Senate. It gives us the French minimum tariff and the treatment of the most favored nation, on an amount of our products equal to their exportations to us of hides, skins, sugar and molasses. Unfortunately for us. neither France nor her colonies have sent us a great deal of these articles. Still, we are able to secure in exchange reduced rates for some nine or ten millions of our exports ; and for this we took care to select articles wherein we already have some trade established, which a duty discriminating in our favor should develop. We have for France, and for Guadaloupe, Martinique and her other colonies, the whole range of common woods, lumber, clapboards and staves ; canned meats ; fresh, dried and pressed fruits, and hops. These articles have been chosen, as you will see, with a view of affecting large classes of small producers and large sections of the country. We had some other beautiful selections made, but, unfortunately, the trade in them was already so large that it more than filled the bill.

There is another matter on which we have had some talk, and on which I hope for something definite by an early steamer. It is possible that this may lead to a little more reciprocity that shall be mutually beneficial. I betray no confidence, indeed, in saying that the thoughts of French statesmen. in and out of the Government, are turning, in the present economical condition of their country, more and more toward some general reciprocal arrangement with the United States. Some suggestions that came to me on this subject could not, perhaps, be properly detailed here ; but there can be no harm, I think, in quoting a remark made to me more than once by the President of the last Chamber, and the President now of the Chamber's Tariff Commission, M. MELINE, who is, more than any one other, the author of the new tariff—the Major McKINLEY, in fact, of France. Said he : ''One of the first things I should favor, after the workings of our tariff are known, would be a complete commercial treaty with the United States." [Applause.]

This is a matter, however, in which the assent of the legislative bodies on both sides the water would be required; and when I recall the trials of pork, and the entirely unsentimental view both countries take of trade problems, I am not sure that the lot of the Minister who is fortunate enough to negotiate that treaty will be an altogether happy one.

In any case, the trade situation of France for the next few years is sure to be peculiar and most interesting. She is just entering upon an untried economical *régime*. She has become overwhelmingly Protectionist—no doubt, in part, because of our example—and in one respect she is bettering our instructions with a vengeance. We have generally reached our present high duties by successive steps, often extending throughout a century. France has suddenly, upon dozens of important products, doubled or trebled, even quadrupled, her late duties at a single blow. What is to be the effect upon her trade relations? That is a problem on which it is not wise to dogmatize beforehand; but one or two of its elements seem clear. In this sharp and sudden advance on her old duties, France has gone on our road faster, if not farther, than ourselves, while she must remain under the influence of radically different conditions. Practically speaking, the United States has no neighbors and no frontiers, and it preserves within its own borders, from side to side of the continent and from the lakes to the Gulf, the largest and most beneficent example of absolute Free Trade the world can yet show. France has no continent for such a commerce, no room for four or five times her present population, no such undeveloped opportunities for mining, manufacturing and trade. Now, hemmed in as she is by Spain, Italy, Switzerland, Germany and Belgium, and with but a strip of water like Long Island Sound (though some travellers say a trifle more turbulent) between her and Great Britain—whether thus situated France can successfully adapt our practice to her conditions is a question which her statesmen are not sure of, and to which the leading journals of her capital would generally, at the present, reply in the negative. [Applause.]

In any case, we shall have plenty of trade with her, and, I hope, a growing trade. There is every reason for it. Each country produces at the best what the other wants. France must buy our raw materials and certain of our manufactures. We must buy the finest and most artistic things in the world, whatever they cost, and it is France that makes them. Who supposes that you could stop American women from buying French gowns, fine silks, ribbons and articles de Paris; or American men from buying French pictures and bronzes and tapestries, Bordeaux and champagnes, even if a dozen McKINLEYS stood in the way? We'll grumble about the price, of course; why shouldn't we? but we'll buy all the same.

And all the time, till France loses her secret—the secret of doing the finest things just a little better than anybody else in the world can do them. We know the commercial value of it now; some day, perhaps, we may learn the secret for ourselves. But it will not be till we have learned another lesson—to wit, that the diffusion of art is not merely a luxury, but a commercial necessity; that free art is as vital as free air, and that the country which burdens or which even doesn't cherish and encourage and diffuse art is hopelessly doomed to remain second-class all its years.

We all believe that within this generation New-York is to be the financial and possibly the commercial centre of the world. With all my heart, I hope so. But we must never make the stupid mistake of underrating our rivals; and it is, perhaps, needful also to guard against the natural tendency of a young and prosperous community to overrate themselves. Whatever our natural endowments, or whatever the genius of our people, we are always in danger whenever we shut our eyes to the experience of the world.

Our friends, the French, are, at this moment, enormously prosperous—probably the most prosperous nation in Europe ; and with their prosperity, the most widely diffused. And yet, when I contrast the French condition with ours, when I recall our own popular grievances—as to railroads, for example—and remember that there is not in all France a train to be compared to those on which you daily travel to Washington or Chicago—that no money can there purchase equal luxury, and that what you can purchase costs you double as much per mile; or when I recall another of our grievances as to the cost of living, and referring to my cash book, am reminded that Paris, to a foreign Minister, at any rate, and I think to Americans generally, is as dear as New-York, if not dearer, I wonder if occasionally our national complaints may not spring less from the acuteness of our sufferings than from the acuteness of our politics. [Applause.]

We shall be on exhibition next year in Chicago, and here too. It may not be a mistake to assume that among other things the merchants of New-York will wish to show their foreign guests will be a dollar which. following the thought of the President, is as good as any other dollar the country has issued, a navy no longer ridiculous, and streets and a judiciary for which we have no occasion to apologize. [Applause.]

The French are coming, not exactly in squadrons, perhaps, but in larger numbers than they have ever travelled before. They are coming to a land in which they believe their welcome is ready, and I am sure you will make it so. They will teach this generation of Americans how, in her sphere, France still leads the world. She will come to the nation she helped to create as our old ally ; better still, she will come as the great sister Republic. She will come, as I ventured to predict in Paris, even before the action of the Chambers on the appropriation, as France ought to come to America—on the front line, and with all her banners flying. She will show what higher development the country has reached under the Republic, and in the stirring language of her own Ministers, she will carry to this new Western centre, in which the progress of civilization now asserts itself, the shining proofs of the activity and the genius of her children. [Applause.]

Our hearts will go out to her, I am sure, as to none else. We hold in high honor that upright and most successful statesman and that model citizen, the President of the Republic, M. CARNOT. We know how faithfully and how ably the country is served under him by RIBOT and DE FREYCINET, by JULES ROCHE, by TIRARD and SPULLER, by ROYER and FLOQUET, and their colleagues in the Ministry and in the Chambers : and the earnest desire of our people, without distinction of parties and without dissent—I have said it as your Minister in France, and I wish to say it as the guest of the Chamber of Commerce in New-York—the desire of our whole people is, that under their wise guidance and that of their successors, the Republic, which has now become the strongest as it is the oldest government France has had for a century, may endure throughout the generations of men, and that it may mean always, as it means now, order and prosperity for the French, and peace for Europe. [Prolonged applause.]

THE PRESIDENT.—Gentlemen, the next regular toast is : "THE PRESS." It is eminently fitting and proper that this powerful exponent of public opinion should be represented upon this occasion by the learned and eloquent Nestor of New-York Journalism. I now have the peculiar pleasure of calling on the Hon. CHARLES A. DANA to respond for his profession. [Applause.]

MR. CHAIRMAN AND GENTLEMEN : I cannot imagine that there is any occasion for any representative of the press to arise here, after Mr. REID has taken his seat. Who can speak for the press so well as he? Who has had an experience so wide, so varied, so creditable, so successful as he? There was in the earlier history of this Republic a school of thinkers who held that diplomacy was comparatively unnecessary ; that we should have no foreign ministers except upon special occasions, when they might be sent out to settle some pressing controversy, and then come home, leaving the country without any representative except its consuls in foreign lands. That school was never very extensive. So far as I am aware its principal members were two men of different parties and most distinguished genius. One of them, THOMAS H. BENTON, a great and broad-minded statesman of the earlier days of our political life ; and the other was another man of genius. HORACE GREELEY. [Laughter and applause.]

They both taught this doctrine, and taught it with such ability and such success that they made at least one convert, and at an early age I entered their school myself. [Laughter.] I also know of one other newspaper man who belonged to the school, but it never was a successful party ; it never got any standing in the world ; the American people never adopted the idea, and why? Well, in the first place, there is a kind of politeness and good society among nations which requires that every power, every nation of any consequence, should have its regular representatives near the governments of other nations. That is a kind of international good manners which the world has never been willing to resign.

We all agree—I have joined the other side, I have gone over to the majority, [applause,]—we all agree that diplomatic representatives and ministers maintained permanently abroad are indispensable for the good conduct of international affairs. Another consideration also bears upon this question. There are certain offices, certain political and public functions which are indispensable to the conduct of society. There must be governors, there must be legislators, there must be judges, there must be tax collectors—all those functions are absolutely necessary, and they are maintained as a matter of necessity. But the catalogue of public offices is not complete with those indispensable functionaries. It has to go further.

We must have officers who, under certain circumstances and to a certain extent, are ornamental. There must be places of importance for public men of distinction. They cannot all be elected judges, or lieutenant-governors, or members of Congress, or Senators; there must be other places to which, when a new President comes into power, he can send distinguished men of his own party, and he ought not to send any other, [applause,] to foreign lands as the representatives of the Government and of the power and dignity of the United States.

For a great part of the time these foreign representatives of ours may have very little to do; but it is indispensable, I think, to have them there, and when the occasion arises, when there is a need, when there is some important question to be settled, then we must have them there; and unless they are there with some antecedents, and some experience, and some knowledge of the medium in which they have to labor, and of the men with whom they have to deal, their efforts would be comparatively ineffectual and useless. So we have for all these reasons come over to the doctrine that there must be a diplomatic establishment maintained by the United States.

Now, we do not maintain it as other countries do. The old Governments make diplomacy a profession; men are educated to it; they make their careers in it; they follow that business all their lives through. Here we do not do it that way, for the reason that this is a Government of change; that it is a Government in which men pass from one sphere of life to another, in which they are promoted according to their deserts; so that we, instead of educating our diplomats to be diplomats, put them early in life in newspaper offices, and when they graduate we have something brilliant and admirable. [Laughter and applause.]

The honors which you are paying to our distinguished fellow-citizen, Mr. REID, this evening, are not only well deserved, but, as has been remarked, they are paid in substance by all parties in this country. [Applause.] When you can get not merely a Republican like my friend, Mr. SMITH, and a celebrated Mugwump, like my friend, Mr. COUDERT, [laughter,] and modest and unpretentious democrats, like Senator BRICE and myself, [laughter,] to come here and join in the honor; and when General SCHURZ, the greatest Mugwump of them all, comes, [laughter,] and when they all combine in paying this well-deserved tribute to a distinguished and successful public servant, we may be sure that the honor is perfectly deserved; and that greater services hereafter may be expected from the gentleman who has rendered them. [Applause.]

The fact is, that there is not any important public service that a successful newspaper man is not perfectly well able to render on the shortest notice. [Laughter and applause.] The foundation of success such as Mr. REID has achieved is considerably made up of that good fortune which is apt to befall men of superior ability

and judgment. It is not merely talent; it is not merely
devotion to the duty undertaken ; it is not merely the
concentration of every faculty ; but after all, this good
luck comes into it. Such good luck I look to see
further illustrated in the case of our distinguished
guest of this evening. [Applause.] The past at least
is secure. [Applause.] That is a common saying, but
the past is always a pointer to the future, and these distinctions, outside of those strictly belonging to the
newspaper press, may be placed upon Mr. REID hereafter, as the laurel is placed upon the head of a great and
successful soldier. We shall feel, we who belong to the
newspaper press, whether in the capacity of retired
members, like General SCHURZ, or active members, like
my friend, Mr. HALSTEAD, or occasional contributors,
like my friend, Mr. COUDERT, [laughter,] we shall all
feel that a part of the honor and a part of the renown
belongs to the profession of which Mr. REID is so distinguished a member. [Applause.]

THE PRESIDENT.—Gentlemen, the next and last
regular toast is: "MODERN DIPLOMACY, THE ALLY OF
COMMERCE." I think we have had a very happy illus-
tration of the truth of this sentiment in the life and
character of our friend and guest this evening. [Ap-
plause.] The gentleman who will respond to this toast
needs no introduction to this assemblage. I have great
pleasure in calling upon General HORACE PORTER.
[Applause.]

SPEECH OF GENERAL HORACE PORTER.

MONSIEUR LE PRESIDENT ET MESSIEURS : Si je
m'adresse à vous ce soir dans une langue que je ne parle
pas et que personne ici ne comprend, j'en impute la
faute entièrement a mon ami, l'ex-ministre, car on me
dit que depuis son retour il a oublié tout son Français

et il ne pent plus parler Anglais, et c'est tres embarras-
sant. [Laughter and applause.]

A friend by my side tells me that, notwithstanding
the short time which has elapsed since our Minister's
return, he has succeeded in catching up with enough
English to understand me fairly well, in that tongue,
provided I speak loud. [Laughter.] And yet I always
like to speak in a foreign language where there are no
foreigners present. [Renewed laughter.] It invariably
calls down less adverse criticism on one's accent.
[Laughter.]

I am exceedingly glad to participate in a dinner given
to a gentleman upon his return home. We have usually
been engaged in giving dinners to gentlemen upon the
eve of their departure from home, in which there always
seems to be an implied condition that the guest shall
leave the country within twenty-four hours thereafter.
[Laughter.] Less than two years ago I started to Eu
rope to visit Mr. REID, in the hope that I might get
from him a straight tip in diplomacy. I found a great
many public men going over to Europe about the same
time. Our public men seem to think that they will add
greatly to their public reputation in crossing the water,
particularly when they consider how much it added to
the reputation of GEORGE WASHINGTON even crossing
the Delaware River. [Great laughter.] On my arrival
abroad I immediately began the study of the difference
between the French race and our English race. The
real difference did not strike me until I crossed the English Channel. The last man I saw in England was a
soldier, with his red coat and his blue trousers. The first
man I saw on my landing in France was a soldier, with
his blue coat and red trousers, and I said to myself,
"That settles it; when you turn a Frenchman upside
down he becomes an Englishman." [Roars of laughter.]

On my arrival in Paris I found that the people had
adopted many of our customs, and our English phrases

descriptive of them. A French friend, wanting to invite me to take tea with him in the afternoon, said : "Voulez-vous 5 o'clocker, avec moi?" and I replied : "Yes, with a great deal of pleasure ; at what hour?" He said to me : "You seem to understand everything I say except my English." [Laughter.]

Then I visited the Chamber of Deputies. I found that body vociferous. A deputy made a motion, and immediately all the other deputies arose, howled, upset piles of books, yelled and tried to jerk the benches loose from the floor. I supposed they were mutinying, but I was mistaken ; they were only coinciding in the motion. [Laughter.] Then I saw on the opposite bank of the river from the Chamber of Deputies that most beautiful of all street scenes, the Place de la Concorde, and a gentleman of a philosophic turn of mind said : "Here we have the Place de la Concorde opposite the place de la discorde. [Renewed laughter.]

Everybody in France was excited on the subject of the tariff ; and I was somewhat surprised to find the familiarity with which they continually spoke of our Ohio statesman. They were constantly alluding to "Ze Bill McKinley." I told them that it was only a matter of taste : that in this country we usually spoke of him as William. [Great laughter.]

The American hog was in every Frenchman's mind, but that did not suit the grasping disposition of our exporters ; they wanted to have it in everybody's stomach. [Renewed laughter.] They were attacking the American hog in all directions, and I saw that he was not having a fair show. Every disease, from cerebro spinal meningitis to interstertial nephritis was attributed to a lack of health in the American hog. They had an exaggerated idea of the hog in America. They believed that the people in Chicago found lard oil light cheaper than daylight, and that the merchants closed their stores in the daytime and burned lard oil lamps for the sake of economy. [Laughter.] Whenever they heard of a man in Paris who was from Chicago they went to testing the matter by feeling for the bristles on his back. [Renewed laughter.]

Now I do not like to see the American hog abused. He had been a friend of ours in the army. I have many a time helped to slaughter him and eat him in all his various phases of health. [Laughter.] In an army you may get tired of horse meat, and mule meat, even of good beef, but you never get tired of pork. The only trouble you are likely to have in an army is getting enough of it. When the men seized upon a hog on the march, they never stopped in order to slaughter him. The boys got to be so expert, that they could skin him, quarter him, and slice him up without ever slackening their gait or losing the step.

It is popularly supposed that the hog is not a discriminating animal, but he is very particular and self-examining. If he supposes that his sanitary condition is not sound, he tests the matter—he sticks his tail in a pot of a water, and watches it boil. When he finds himself entitled to a clean bill of health, he uses that same tail to point with pride to his robust condition.

The French need no longer appoint government inspectors to examine the American hog. He can inspect himself much more intelligently. He is sensitive, however, in regard to having duties imposed upon him. Like the human species, he does not like to be imposed upon, especially by foreigners. He feels that Mr. REID has befriended him manfully. [Great laughter.]

Mr. REID secured France as the first nation to ratify our international copyright act, and the first nation to reduce the prohibitory duty on pork. In both instances he was eminently successful in securing justice for the products of the pen. [Laughter.]

I enjoyed a number of very elaborate dinners at Mr. REID's house, and I have a lively recollection that the

list of courses was longer than LEPORELLO's list of all of
DON GIOVANNI's sweethearts. I read some time after
of a man who died from a foreign growth in the stomach,
and I said, "That man has been eating one of REID's
dinners." [Laughter.]

And now, in behalf of Americans who have sojourned
abroad, I wish to make the most grateful acknowledg-
ments for the attention, courtesy and hospitality which
they invariably received from Mr. REID while they tar-
ried in that foreign land. He does not fully realize how
much heartsease he planted in their gardens. [Ap-
plause.] As Americans we have all had reason to feel
justly proud of his triumphant career as an American
diplomatist. Scarcely had he reached France when the
most complicated, intricate and difficult problems in
diplomacy were presented to him for solution ; and it is
a great gratification for us to be able to say that in
bringing order out of chaos, in regard to American ex-
hibits at the Paris Exposition, in securing France as the
first nation to ratify our International Copyright act,
the first nation to accept our invitation to the Columbus
Exposition, in negotiating an admirable extradition
treaty, in carrying through a most important plan for
reciprocity, and in the inestimable benefit he conferred
upon American industries by his complete success in
securing the removal of the prohibitory duties upon
American pork, he has never once lowered the dignity
of his country ; he has maintained throughout the entire period the confidence of his Government, and by his
firmness, tact and sense of justice, has commanded the
cordial sympathy and respect of the Government to
which he was accredited. It was exceedingly gratifying
to have us represented by such a man in France ; to
have his efforts successful in increasing the cordial relations which exist between the oldest Republic of the
New World and the youngest Republic of the Old
World. [Applause.]

There is something more than mere sentiment which has arisen from the circumstances which surrounded the French Alliance. In the darkest hours of our revolution, when hope seemed fading and confidence waning, a light broke in upon us from the eastern horizon. That light came from the generous land of France. [Applause.] From that time forth, when we saw upon the field GATES and GREENE, and PUTNAM and WASHINGTON, we saw standing by their side, D'ESTAING, ROCHAMBEAU, and that knightly, princely warrior, the immortal LAFAYETTE. [Applause and cheers.] ARIOSTO tells a beautiful story of a gentle fairy, who, by a singular dispensation, was required at times to assume the form of a grovelling serpent and crawl upon the earth. Those who spurned her and trampled upon her when in this abject state, were deprived of the precious gifts that it was in her power to bestow, but those who comforted, encouraged and aided her, found her always standing with arms outstretched pouring her princely gifts into their laps. And now that America has risen in her might, has shaken off the garb of infancy and stands erect, clothed in the robes of majesty and power in which GOD intends her henceforth to tread the earth, she always stands with arms outstretched to France in token of the gratitude she bears her. [Applause and cheers.]

THE PRESIDENT.—Gentlemen, the Chair finds himself at this moment surrounded by an embarrassment of riches. We have finished the regular programme, and volunteer toasts are now in order. I find on my right a distinguished president of a great college, and also a distinguished clergyman of a great church. We have in our company an ex-mayor of New-York, who is also a distinguished ex-member of Congress. I have refrained from calling any of these gentlemen by name, but I am sure you will select one or all of them to speak to you.

Calls were then made for President Low, of Columbia College, and in response, he spoke as follows.

SPEECH OF PRESIDENT SETH LOW, OF COLUMBIA COLLEGE.

MR. CHAIRMAN AND GENTLEMEN: General PORTER, I am sure, will not consider it any discredit to the Latin with which he begun his recent eloquent speech, if I say that it reminded me of a recent conversation between a sophomore and a freshman at Columbia College. The freshman appealed to his elder brother with this query: " What is the French for eau de vie?" and the sophomore replied that he was not quite sure, but he thought it was eau sucré [Laughter.] A few evenings ago it became my duty to try to explain this phenomenon of nature. I found myself at a dinner given to Sir EDWIN ARNOLD, and the question naturally arose, how could it be that the poet and the editor could exist in the same person? The explanation suggested was, that in these days editor and poet alike live upon their imagination. [Laughter.] To-night I am obliged to hazard a conjecture as to how it is that an editor and a diplomatist can exist in the same person? I think far too highly of the press to intimate that that could be the explanation which TALLEYRAND suggested, that the art of using language by a diplomatist was to use words so as to conceal your thoughts. [Laughter.] I think, rather, that the historian hit upon the correct explanation, when he said of a certain historical character of the Middle Ages, that he discomfited all the diplomatists of his time simply by telling the truth. [Laughter.] What is more natural and more characteristic of the newspaper editor than that?

And yet, by way of explanation of the particular phenomenon which concerns and interests us to-night, Mr. Chairman, why it is that our distinguished guest and fellow-countryman has been so great a success as a diplomatist, I can contribute one item of information. You heard him say, we all heard him say, how, in that position, the greatness of the country entered into his veins, and all the dignity and the power of this great people stirred and animated his heart ; but they did not make him great beyond sympathy with the small and the unknown. [Applause.] It came to me to send a couple of our younger students to his care, asking that he would secure for them access to the great libraries of France. He not only did that, he not only placed his official services at their disposition, but he treated them with a personal courtesy that won their hearts and the admiration of the university to which they belonged. [Applause.] With this consciousness of the greatness of the country, he remembered its attitude of honoring the small and the inconspicuous, and I think that is one reason why Mr. REID distinguished himself as an American Minister at the Court of France. [Applause.]

Mr. Chairman, in the days when it was my pleasure to be in business life, I had many dealings with France, and particularly in connection with the manufacture and importation of silks, or rather with the importation of raw silks for manufacture here ; and I used to think that no one feature, no one element, had contributed more to the progress of manufacturers in this country than the teachableness that was characteristic of our men. They would learn from Lyons and from Zurich with equal open-mindedness. They imitated the pat-terns, they dissected the cloth, and so the manufacture here made wonderful progress.

But Mr. REID has pointed out one thing that we have still to learn, that is, perhaps, of more importance than any material lesson which France can teach us. I asked how many men one of these manufacturers in Paterson employed, on one occasion, and he told me that there were, in his employ, so many hundred hands. When I reached Lyons I found that they called those hands, "artists." [Applause.] That is the reason why France leads the world to day in everything that is beautiful, and that appeals to the universal taste.

I want to point out simply one other thing with regard to her attitude. She throws her art schools open to all the world. [Applause.] She recognizes that there are no artificial boundaries in the domain of art, that truth and beauty are not only eternal, but that they are to be found the world over. [Applause.] I think we must show the same hospitality to art that France displays, before we shall be worthy to stand as a republic in the world of art, side by side with the great Republic of France. [Applause.] I thank the American Minister for taking this occasion of saying to our people, what I hope he will repeat in season and out of season—that he who would be truly great must be willing to meet the world on even terms. [Applause.]

THE PRESIDENT.—Gentlemen, we have a distinguished journalist from the other side of the river, and I know you will be glad to have him say a few words on this occasion. I therefore call upon the Hon. MURAT HAL-STEAD.

SPEECH OF THE HON. MURAT HALSTEAD.

MR. CHAIRMAN : The embarrassment of riches that is upon you makes this, to me, an entirely unexpected pleasure and honor ; the time is so short before the dawn of Easter morning. It was THOMAS JEFFERSON, I believe, who said of the Americans, that they were fortunate in having two countries, one their own and the other France.

Was it HUGO? Well, HUGO borrowed it from JEFFER-

SON as many others borrowed very many other clever things from him. [Laughter.]

The guest whom we honor to-night was fortunate in the time of his ministry to France in finding her restored to her place among the nations of the earth, confident in herself, and again giving to European powers their equilibrium. One of the things which aided France more than anything else, perhaps, to resume her place among the nations was her magnificent Exposition, in which she gave such an example to the world. [Applause.]

It has not been long since it was my privilege to be in Europe and to meet there the American Ministers in several of the great capitals of Europe—Rome, Vienna, Berlin, Paris, London—and more charming and delightful American homes are not to be found anywhere upon our continent than those of the Ministers of the United States representing us in Europe. [Applause.]

It has recently been mentioned that some dispute has arisen about the presumption on the part of Mr. PHELPS, the American Minister to Germany, in regard to some remark of his touching the relations of our country with one of the islands of the sea, and the newspaper press of Germany (we have had so much to say of the press this evening that it seems appropriate to mention it) have taken the matter up with a great deal of vigor and energy, and of apparent animosity, but they do not care for that matter at all ; that which concerns them is, that the policy of the United States and her commercial growth is taking from Germany a great deal of the influence that she has heretofore exerted in South America, and they are fearing we shall get the usufruct of that trade and great influence which they, themselves, have enjoyed. They are scolding on general principles.

I have had very often much sympathy with our guest of this evening. We were born in the same State in the Miami country, and have known each other long and well ; and there is one thing, and one only, that I will undertake to say here and now, touching his relations abroad, the one thing that has been, in some degree, neglected ; and yet that seems to me the most important and most distinguished of all his honorable distinctions, and that was that he recognized from the first, in France, the fact that he was the representative of a Republican Government and that France was a republic, and his constant sympathy, as I know, was with the republicanism of that great nation, in which all Europe is interested, and in which we take just and laudable pride. [Applause.]

I have, gentlemen of the Chamber of Commerce of New-York, for forty years known much of this great city, and, as I have become better acquainted with it, there is one institution in this City of New-York that does not decline with close acquaintance, with familiarity with its methods, with a knowledge of the influence that it exerts, the information of the power it wields, and the intellect that it commands, the resources with which it goes forth throughout the globe—there is an institution from which the enchantment has not gone—and that is the grand Chamber of Commerce of the City of New-York. I congratulate my old friend upon the distinguished honor of this reception at your hands—one that I am sure he, with his experience in affairs of the world, prizes most highly and esteems as the crowning honor of his career in diplomacy so happily terminated, and his entrance upon new duties at home that are so promising in regard to the future. [Applause.]

When Mr. HALSTEAD had completed his speech the President announced the conclusion of the proceedings. The company then separated.

LETTERS RECEIVED.

Among the letters received from gentlemen invited to the Banquet, and·who were prevented from attending, were the following :

FROM BENJAMIN HARRISON, PRESIDENT OF THE UNITED STATES.

EXECUTIVE MANSION,
WASHINGTON, *April* 11, 1892.

Hon. CHAUNCEY M. DEPEW and others,
Committee, &c.

GENTLEMEN : I am very sorry that I cannot accept the invitation of the Chamber of Commerce of the State of New-York to attend the Banquet to be given to Hon. WHITELAW REID on the evening of Saturday, the 16th inst. There are controlling reasons of a public and private character that will prevent my leaving Washington at the time indicated. I am glad to notice that New-York so gracefully and fully recognizes the important services which Mr. REID has been able to render to this country during his residence in Paris as United States Minister, and would be glad to participate with the members of the Chamber of Commerce in the expression of this feeling if it were possible.

Very truly yours,
(Signed,)   BENJ. HARRISON.

FROM EX-PRESIDENT RUTHERFORD B. HAYES.

FIFTH AVENUE HOTEL, MADISON SQUARE,
NEW-YORK, 14*th April*, 1892.

GENTLEMEN : In full sympathy with your purpose to

recognize the services of Mr. REID in France, I am, with regret, compelled by my engagements to deny myself the pleasure of accepting your invitation for Saturday evening.

Sincerely,

(Signed,) RUTHERFORD B. HAYES.

Messrs. DEPEW, PORTER, BLISS, BABCOCK, ORR,
Committee.

FROM EX-PRESIDENT GROVER CLEVELAND.

Mr. GROVER CLEVELAND regrets that he is unable to accept the courteous invitation of the Chamber of Commerce of the State of New-York to attend a Banquet to be given to the Hon. WHITELAW REID, Minister of the United States to France, on the 16th instant.

LAKEWOOD, N. J., *April* 8, 1892.

FROM THE HON. LEVI P. MORTON, VICE-PRESIDENT OF THE UNITED STATES.

VICE-PRESIDENT'S CHAMBER,
WASHINGTON, *April* 11*th*, 1892.

DEAR SIR: I regret that the expected absence of Senator MANDERSON, President *pro tempore* of the Senate, will deprive me of the pleasure of availing myself of the invitation of the Chamber of Commerce to be present at the Banquet to be given the Hon. WHITELAW REID on the 16th instant. Again regretting my inability to join with my fellow-members of the Chamber in extending hearty congratulations to Mr. REID upon the successful results of his mission,

I am, very truly yours,

(Signed,) LEVI P. MORTON.

Hon. CORNELIUS BLISS,
Chairman Committee of Arrangements.

FROM THE HON. BENJAMIN F. TRACY, SECRETARY OF
THE NAVY.

NAVY DEPARTMENT, WASHINGTON.

Mr. BENJAMIN F. TRACY regrets exceedingly that he
will be unable to accept the very kind invitation of the
Chamber of Commerce to attend the Banquet to be given
to Hon. WHITELAW REID on Saturday evening, the
16th inst.

April 11*th*, 1892.

FROM THE HON. JOHN W. NOBLE, SECRETARY OF THE
INTERIOR.

DEPARTMENT OF THE INTERIOR,
WASHINGTON, *April* 11*th*, 1892.

MY DEAR SIR: On the afternoon of Saturday, the
16th instant, I have an engagement at the Fifth Avenue
Hotel to meet my brethren of the fraternity of the Beta
Theta Pi, and thereby am prevented from accepting
your very kind invitation to the Banquet to Hon.
WHITELAW REID, Minister of the United States to
France, given by the Chamber of Commerce of the
State of New-York, at DELMONICO'S, on the same
evening.

Nothing would give me greater pleasure than to bear
my tribute of respect to our eminent fellow-citizen, who
has so faithfully and successfully performed the duties
of the office entrusted to him.

American commerce has been greatly promoted and
our friendly relations have been signally advanced, not
only with France, but with other countries, by his
labors.

It gives me pleasure to add that, from the testimony
of many who have met Mr. REID abroad, though
engaged in the onerous duties devolved upon him, he

has at all times shown the utmost consideration for our
fellow-citizens abroad, and proved himself in private
affairs as well as in public a patriotic American.

With the best wishes for the success of your enter-
tainment, I remain,

Most respectfully,
(Signed,)   JOHN W. NOBLE.

Mr. CORNELIUS N. BLISS,
> *Chairman Banquet Committee,*
> *Chamber of Commerce,*
> *New-York.*

FROM MR. CHIEF-JUSTICE FULLER, UNITED STATES
SUPREME COURT.

The Chief-Justice begs to acknowledge the invitation
of the Chamber of Commerce of the State of New-York
to be present at the Banquet to the Hon. WHITELAW
REID, Minister of the United States to France, at
DELMONICO'S, on Saturday evening, April 16th, at half-
past six o'clock, and to express his regret that official
duties here will prevent his participating in this mani-
festation of the appreciation of the service rendered by
Mr. REID to his country in promoting its commercial
interests while discharging the duties of that high
position.

WASHINGTON, *April 8th,* 1892.

FROM THE HON. JOHN SHERMAN.

SENATE CHAMBER, WASHINGTON,
April 8th, 1892.

CORNELIUS N. BLISS, Esq., Chairman.

MY DEAR SIR: I have the honor to acknowledge
receipt of the invitation of the Chamber of Commerce
to attend their Banquet to the Hon. WHITELAW
REID, Minister of the United States to France. It

would give me great pleasure to evince in this way my appreciation of the service rendered by Mr. REID, and the great benefit he has conferred upon his countrymen by his wise, sagacious and liberal course during his important mission in promoting the commercial interests of the United States, but my public duties here will not permit me to do so.

Very respectfully yours,

(Signed,)   JOHN SHERMAN.

FROM THE HON. CHARLES F. CRISP, SPEAKER OF THE HOUSE OF REPRESENTATIVES.

SPEAKER'S ROOM,
HOUSE OF REPRESENTATIVES, WASHINGTON, D. C.,
April 8th, 1892.

Hon. CORNELIUS N. BLISS, *Chairman Banquet Committee, Chamber of Commerce, N. Y.*

MY DEAR SIR: I beg to acknowledge the receipt of your kind invitation to the Banquet to be given to the Hon. WHITELAW REID, Minister to France, on the 16th instant, and regret very much that my engagements here are such that it will be impossible for me to accept it.

Yours very respectfully,

(Signed,)   CHARLES F. CRISP.

FROM THE HON. THOMAS F. BAYARD.

Mr. BAYARD has the honor to acknowledge the invitation of the Chamber of Commerce of the State of New-York to the Banquet to be given to the Hon. WHITELAW REID, on April the 16th, at DELMONICO'S, and regrets that a previous engagement prevents his acceptance.

WILMINGTON, DELAWARE, *April 8th*, 1892.

FROM THE HON. ROBERT R. HITT.

HOUSE OF REPRESENTATIVES,
WASHINGTON, *April* 12, 1892.

Hon. CORNELIUS N. BLISS, Chairman, &c.

DEAR SIR: I have been trying to so arrange that I might accept your bidding for Saturday to meet you at dinner and join the Chamber of Commerce in greeting WHITELAW REID. But it is impossible—engagements and duties prevent it.

He did much for America and Americans. He pressed wider open the doors for our commerce in everything, as coming years and increasing returns will show, for which the Chamber of Commerce of New-York may well testify appreciation; but the West has a special and grateful satisfaction in his success in securing the re-admission, after a long taboo, of "the short and simple animal of the poor." This is a great, substantial fact, with solid results already felt. The immense difficulties and powerful resistance overcome I can well appreciate, knowing the strong interest of the great agricultural proprietors and their compact organization and political power in the Chamber of Deputies, which, during the first administration of President GRÉVY, when we thought we were on the eve of success and had already obtained a decree from the Executive, thwarted all our efforts by the action of the Chamber. The skill, the untiring patience and discreet activity with which his triumph was won mark him as one of the worthiest in the long line of illustrious men who have filled the French Mission, and prove again that America can, without the training of a diplomatic career, produce one whose abilities, tried by the severe test of success, place them in the very front rank of diplomatists.

Very truly yours,
(Signed,)   ROBERT R. HITT.

FROM MR. J. PATENÖTRE, ENVOY EXTRAORDINARY AND
MINISTER PLENIPOTENTIARY OF FRANCE.

LEGATION DE FRANCE, AUX ETATS UNIS,
WASHINGTON, 6th April, 1892.

SIR: I hasten to thank you for the very great kindness
of your invitation to the Banquet, on the 16th of April,
to the Hon. WHITELAW REID. Unhappily it will be
impossible for me to accept it, as I am unavoidably
occupied at that date by other engagements. I regret
all the more not to be able to accept your very gracious
hospitality, because the personal relations between
myself and your Minister at Paris has always been most
agreeable, and I am very much pained not to be able to
be present at New-York upon the interesting occasion.

Accept, sir, the assurance of my distinguished consideration.

(Signed,) PATENÖTRE.

To Mr. CHARLES S. SMITH,
President of the Chamber of Commerce, Y. N.

FROM GOVERNOR ROSWELL P. FLOWER.

STATE OF NEW-YORK,
EXECUTIVE CHAMBER, ALBANY.

Governor FLOWER presents his compliments to the
Chamber of Commerce of the State of New-York, and
regrets that, owing to his engagements already made for
that time, he is unable to accept their kind invitation to
attend the Banquet to be given in honor of the Hon.
WHITELAW REID, at DELMONICO'S, on Saturday evening,
April 16th.

April 15th, 1892.

FROM THE HON. WILLIAM M. EVARTS.

231 SECOND AVENUE.

GENTLEMEN : I have had the honor to receive the

invitation of the Chamber of Commerce to attend a public Banquet to be given in honor of Minister WHITE-LAW REID on Saturday, the 16th inst.

I most heartily appreciate the eminent services to the country rendered by Mr. REID, in the commercial and other great interests, in his conduct of his important mission during the last three years as our diplomatic representative in France. It is but a just tribute to these great public services which the Chamber of Commerce proposes to pay to our distinguished citizen, and in which the cordial sentiments of all our people will find their just expression.

I regret, however, to feel that the impaired condition of my eyesight precludes me from taking part in public assemblages, and with my sincere wishes for the prosperity of this noteworthy celebration, and with my thanks for the attention shown me by the invitation of the Chamber, I am, gentlemen,

Very respectfully,

Your obedient servant,

(Signed,)   WM. M. EVARTS.

CORNELIUS N. BLISS, Esq.,
Chairman of Committee.

FROM THE HON. HAMILTON FISH.

NEW-YORK, *April 8th*, 1892,

251 East Seventeenth Street.

To THE CHAMBER OF COMMERCE OF THE STATE OF NEW-YORK.

GENTLEMEN: I have the honor to acknowledge the invitation to the Banquet to the Hon. WHITELAW REID, to be given on April 16th. It would afford me much pleasure to join in this well-merited tribute to Mr. REID's valuable service to the country, but the condition of my health compels me to deny myself the pleasure.

I am, very respectfully,

(Signed,) HAMILTON FISH.

FROM THE HON. FREDERICK W. SEWARD.

MONTROSE, N. Y.,
April 11th, 1892.

GENTLEMEN : More than a dozen years ago, when a high diplomatic position was offered to Mr. REID, he declined it ; wisely, I thought, because his great journalistic enterprise then needed his personal presence and attention. When, during the present Administration, the Government again sought his aid in affairs abroad, the *Tribune* had become so thoroughly organized and assured of success that he could accept the proffered honor. So, in fact, he has been serving his country on both sides of the Atlantic at once—as journalist and as diplomatist. How well and faithfully his diplomatic labors have been performed is now a matter of historic record. He has rendered eminent service in promoting the interests of American commerce in Europe, as well as in strengthening the traditional friendship between France and the United States, which dates back to the very beginning of our Republic, and I trust may continue to its end.

Your welcome to him on his return is a deserved recognition and tribute. I regret that other engagements will deprive me of the pleasure of sharing in it.

Very respectfully yours,

(Signed,) FREDERICK W. SEWARD.

Messrs. CORNELIUS N. BLISS., &c., &c., &c.

FROM THE HON. GEORGE WILLIAM CURTIS.

WEST NEW-BRIGHTON,
STATEN ISLAND, N. Y., *April 11th*, 1892.

MY DEAR SIR: I beg to acknowledge the invitation of the Chamber of Commerce to the Banquet in honor of Mr. WHITELAW REID, and I regret sincerely my inability to accept it. It is most fitting that the ancient and honorable institution which has so long represented with the highest character and dignity the commercial interest of New-York should pay a tribute of respect to the distinguished citizen who, as Minister in France, has served with such eminent ability the interests both of New-York and of the country. As a fellow-craftsman of Mr. REID in the press, I share its pride in the distinction of so eminent an associate, and join heartily in welcoming his return " to drink delight of battle " with the eager host he knows so well.

Very respectfully yours,
(Signed,)   GEORGE WILLIAM CURTIS.
Mr. CHARLES S. SMITH, *President.*

FROM THE RIGHT REV. WILLIAM ALEXANDER, D. D.,
BISHOP OF DERRY AND RAPHOE.

EPISCOPAL THEOLOGICAL SCHOOL,
CAMBRIDGE, MASS., *April 9*, 1892.

The Bishop of Derry and Raphoe desires to thank the gentlemen of the Chamber of Commerce for the invitation with which he has been favored to the Banquet to be given to the Hon. WHITELAW REID on Saturday, April 16th.

The Bishop esteems it as the highest honor to have been invited to such a gathering in commemoration of the services of so conspicuous an American citizen, whose name stands high in the ranks of contemporary diplomatists.

But he finds that it will be impossible for him to have the gratification of being present at the Banquet, owing to his engagements.

FROM MR. HENRY WATTERSON.

EVERETT HOUSE,
NEW-YORK, *April* 15, 1892.

MY DEAR SIR: I deeply regret that I am unexpectedly called away, and that I shall not be able to be present to do honor among his neighbors to my old and beloved friend, WHITELAW REID. No man appreciates his private worth more than I do, or has a higher appreciation of his public services. I share to the fullest the spirit of the occasion, and am truly sorry that I cannot personally join in its celebration. With many thanks, dear sir, to you and the Chamber of Commerce for your hospitable and kind invitation,

I am, sincerely,

(Signed,)   HENRY WATTERSON.

The Hon. CORNELIUS N. BLISS, etc., etc.

FROM THE REV. RICHARD S. STORRS, D. D.

80 PIERREPONT STREET, BROOKLYN, N. Y.,
April 11*th*, 1892.

GENTLEMEN : It would give me very great pleasure to accept your kind invitation, and to be present at the Banquet proposed to be given by the Chamber of Commerce to the Honorable WHITELAW REID, in recognition of the recent distinguished services rendered by him as Minister of the United States to France.

I yield to no one in my admiring estimate of the ability and the shining success with which he has discharged the sometimes critical and difficult duties of that high office—laying both nations under almost equal obligation; and if it were possible I should be most happy to join with you, and with those for whom you are acting, in expressing to him in person my special esteem and honor. But the evening selected for the Banquet is one on which I cannot be away from home, and I must hope for some other opportunity to say more fully what in this hurried note can be only briefly and imperfectly suggested.

With great personal regard, and with thanks for your pleasant remembrance of me in connection with an occasion so signal and delightful, I am, gentlemen,

Ever faithfully yours,
(Signed,) R. S. STORRS.

Messrs. CORNELIUS N. BLISS, SAMUEL D. BABCOCK, CHAUNCEY M. DEPEW, HORACE PORTER, ALEXANDER E. ORR.

FROM THE REV. JOHN HALL, D. D.

APRIL 8TH, 1892, 712 FIFTH AVENUE.

CORNELIUS N. BLISS, Esq., Chairman, &c.

MY DEAR SIR: I am sorry that a fixed duty, and a meeting, (on each Saturday night,) will prevent my sharing in the well-deserved honor you propose to our late Minister in Paris. He has done good service in a difficult place, and deserves national recognition.

I am, dear sir, with respect,

Yours most truly,
(Signed,) J. HALL.

FROM MR. GEORGE W. CHILDS.

PHILADELPHIA, April 15, 1892.

MY DEAR MR. BABCOCK: I suppose I am indebted to your kind thoughtfulness for the invitation to the

Chamber of Commerce dinner to Mr. REID. I promptly accepted, and expected much pleasure in being among so many of my old friends, but I find now it will be impossible to be present. Will you please notify the Secretary, so my seat may be filled, perhaps by a better man.

None who will be present to-morrow night can possibly have a higher regard or greater appreciation of Mr. WHITELAW REID than your old friend,

(Signed,)   GEORGE W. CHILDS.

SAMUEL D. BABCOCK, Esq.

FROM VISCOUNT PAUL D'ABZAC, CONSUL-GENERAL OF FRANCE.

CONSULATE-GENERAL DE FRANCE, A NEW-YORK,
4 BOWLING GREEN, *April* 16, 1892.

To the Hon. President of the Chamber of Commerce of the State of New-York, New-York City, N. Y.

SIR: I regret deeply that the condition of my health prevents me from enjoying the courteous invitation the Chamber of Commerce of the State of New-York has extended to me to be one of its guests at the Banquet tendered to the Hon. WHITELAW REID, Minister Plenipotentiary of the United States to France.

I respectfully request you to express to the Chamber of Commerce and to your distinguished guest my sincere regrets at not being among those who will welcome the Hon. WHITELAW REID on his return to his native land after the successful and brilliant achievements of his diplomatic mission, which will be long remembered in France as well as in the United States.

I remain, sir, respectfully yours,

(Signed,)   PAUL D'ABZAC, *Consul-General.*

FROM MR. A. A. LOW, EX-PRESIDENT OF THE CHAMBER OF COMMERCE.

3 PIERREPONT PLACE, BROOKLYN HEIGHTS,
April 12th, 1892.

DEAR SIRS: I have the pleasure to acknowledge receipt of your invitation to be present at the Banquet to be given by the New-York Chamber of Commerce on the 16th inst. to the Hon. WHITELAW REID, Minister of the United States to France, and highly appreciating the honor he has done his country in the discharge of the duties of his high office. I very much regret that I cannot be present on so interesting an occasion, and unite with other members of the Chamber in their tribute of regard.

Respectfully yours,
(Signed,) A. A. LOW.

Messrs. CORNELIUS N. BLISS, CHAUNCEY M. DEPEW, SAMUEL D. BABCOCK, HORACE PORTER, A. E. ORR, *Committee of Arrangements.*

FROM MR. JOSEPH H. CHOATE.

50 WEST FORTY-SEVENTH STREET,
10*th April*, 1892.

MY DEAR MR. BLISS: I regret very much that I am not able to accept the kind invitation of the Chamber of Commerce to the Dinner to be given in honor of Mr. REID on Saturday evening. Mr. REID has rendered such signal service to his country as its representative in France, that he cannot be honored too much or welcomed too warmly on his return.

Yours truly,
(Signed,) JOSEPH H. CHOATE.
Hon. C. N. BLISS.